T0047415

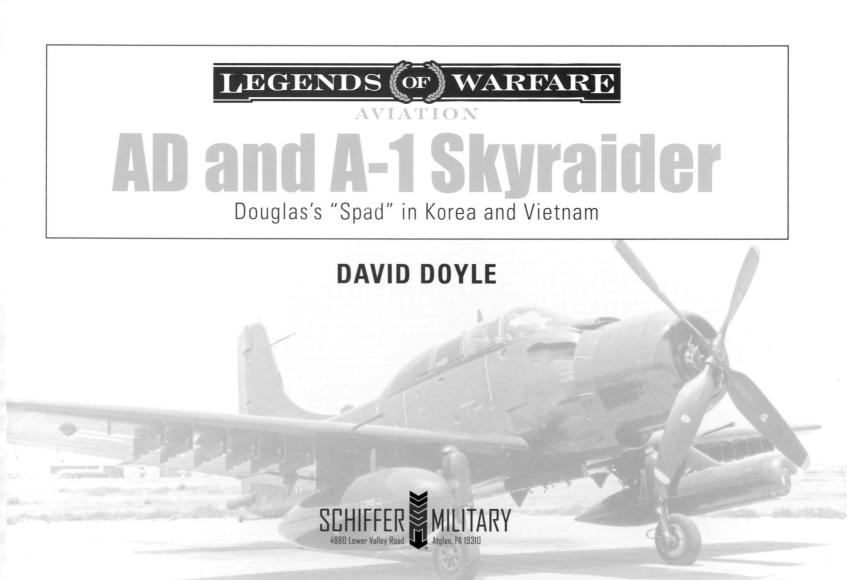

LEGENDS OF WARFARE
AVIATION

AD and A-1 Skyraider

Douglas's "Spad" in Korea and Vietnam

DAVID DOYLE

SCHIFFER MILITARY
4880 Lower Valley Road · Atglen, PA 19310

Copyright © 2021 by David Doyle

Library of Congress Control Number: 2020943395

All rights reserved. No part of this work may be reproduced or used in any form or by any means—graphic, electronic, or mechanical, including photocopying or information storage and retrieval systems—without written permission from the publisher.

The scanning, uploading, and distribution of this book or any part thereof via the Internet or any other means without the permission of the publisher is illegal and punishable by law. Please purchase only authorized editions and do not participate in or encourage the electronic piracy of copyrighted materials.

"Schiffer Military" and the arrow logo are trademarks of Schiffer Publishing, Ltd.

Designed by Justin Watkinson
Type set in Impact/Minion Pro/Univers LT Std
Front cover photo is by Rich Kolasa.

ISBN: 978-0-7643-6132-6
Printed in China

Published by Schiffer Publishing, Ltd.
4880 Lower Valley Road
Atglen, PA 19310
Phone: (610) 593-1777; Fax: (610) 593-2002
E-mail: Info@schifferbooks.com
www.schifferbooks.com

For our complete selection of fine books on this and related subjects, please visit our website at www.schifferbooks.com. You may also write for a free catalog.

Schiffer Publishing's titles are available at special discounts for bulk purchases for sales promotions or premiums. Special editions, including personalized covers, corporate imprints, and excerpts, can be created in large quantities for special needs. For more information, contact the publisher.

We are always looking for people to write books on new and related subjects. If you have an idea for a book, please contact us at proposals@schifferbooks.com.

Acknowledgments

Creating this book has been very much a team effort and could not have been done without a great deal of help from many of my friends. Among those contributing to this effort are Tom Kailbourn, Rich Kolasa, Scott Taylor, and the staffs of the National Museum of Naval Aviation, Naval Historical Center, the National Archives and Records Administration, and the National Museum of the United States Air Force. Through all of this, the Lord has blessed me with a wonderful and supportive wife, without whose encouragement (and scanning!), none of this would be possible. Thank you, Denise!

Photos not otherwise credited are from the National Museum of Naval Aviation.

Contents

Introduction

Skyraider! This dramatic name was well suited to Douglas Aircraft's A-1 attack aircraft. Originally intended for use by the US Navy during the Second World War, the aircraft rolled off the assembly lines too late to take part in the hostilities. It did see action in the Korean War and—well into the jet age—during the war in Vietnam, when it became a weapon in the US Air Force arsenal as well.

Besides the United States, several other countries flew the Skyraider. The British Royal Navy's Fleet Air Arm, France's Armée de l'Air, and the air force of the Republic of Vietnam (South Vietnam, prior to 1975) were among the international services operating the aircraft. The last military to fly the Skyraider in combat was the Groupement Aérien Présidentiel (an air force unit in the West African country of Gabon). France had provided Gabon with eight AD-4N aircraft, and these Skyraiders were not retired until 1985—forty years after the massive propeller-driven fighter first flew.

US servicemen on the ground often have their own unofficial names for the equipment they use, and the Skyraider was no exception. American personnel in Vietnam referred to the anachronistic piston aircraft as a "Spad," borrowing the name of a First World War biplane.

But the story of the Skyraider began long before America's war in Indochina. In 1943, the US Navy was seeking a new plane that could take part both in scouting and torpedo-bomber operations. At the time, the Douglas SBD was fulfilling those functions, but the Navy wanted something with better performance. Douglas Aircraft had been working on its upgraded Dauntless SB2D and had received a contract for two examples of that plane in June 1941, months before Pearl Harbor brought the United States into World War II. By 1943 the Navy's requirements had increased beyond the requirements it had laid down for the SB2D, and Douglas had to make some changes in its design or perhaps even start on something totally new. Douglas improved the existing design to meet the new requirements, including converting the plane to a single-seat configuration, and the new BTD-1 first took to the air in February 1944. The aircraft was still based on older conceptions, however, and Douglas was aware that rival manufacturers were promoting more up-to-date designs—a fact that could mean that the BTD-1 might never receive a contract to go into production. With the aim of discussing progress on the aircraft needed by the Navy, the Bureau of Aeronautics called for a meeting of company representatives from the four aircraft makers that were competing for the contract to build the new torpedo bomber.

Gathering in Washington, DC, the corporate and Navy representatives discussed the situation. Then Ed Heinemann, Douglas's chief engineer, shocked the Navy officials by declaring, "We would like to request that the Navy allow Douglas to cancel the existing contract for the BTD. Instead we ask permission to use the unexpended funds to build an entirely new bomber, one that I am convinced will do the job for you. If you agree, I would like thirty days to draw up and present the design."

Rear Admiral Lawrence Richardson responded almost at once, "All right, Ed, but we can't give you thirty days. You'll have to have a design for us by oh nine hundred tomorrow. And, you'll have to design it around the R-3350. That is a must."

Directly after the meeting, Heinemann telephoned Douglas Aircraft owner Donald Douglas with the news. Heinemann and the other members of the Douglas delegation then went back to newly built Statler Hotel, where they were staying. Fortunately, the Douglas team on hand comprised Leo Devlin, Heinemann's assistant; Reid Bogart, project engineer for the BTD; and Gene Root, an aerodynamicist. The team stayed up into the wee hours of the morning, working until 3:00 a.m. They then grabbed four hours of sleep before returning to the Bureau of Aeronautics with aircraft prints and a proposal. In a few hours the proposal received Navy approval, and the Douglas team headed back to California to get to work on the plan. It was with remarkable speed that the Skyraider was conceived and designed, especially remarkable when the ultimate success of the aircraft is taken into consideration.

Douglas Aircraft built the experimental XSB2D-1 as a potential replacement for that corporation's SBD Dauntless dive-bomber. The SB2D-1 was mounted on a tricycle landing gear. In addition to the pilot, there was an observer/gunner who remotely controlled two machine gun turrets. The dorsal fin was abruptly truncated at the front end to give clearance to the dorsal turret. *San Diego Air and Space Museum*

The Douglas XBTD-1 was an experimental scout and torpedo-bomber aircraft designed to operate in the newly won air-superiority environment of the Pacific war. Its crew consisted solely of the pilot, having neither the defensive machine guns nor the gunner that previously had been a standard feature of US Navy carrier-based scout planes and torpedo bombers. *San Diego Air and Space Museum*

CHAPTER 1
XBT2D-1

In June 1944, when the Navy's Bureau of Aeronautics decided that several competing designs were superior to the Douglas BTD-1, Douglas's chief engineer, Ed Heinemann, and several aides, during an amazing overnight session, designed a completely new aircraft, designated the XBT2D-1 Dauntless II (renamed Skyraider in February 1946), and built around the Wright R-3350 radial engine. Impressed with the concept, the Navy authorized development of the plane. Twenty-five XBT2D-1s were completed. The first one, Bureau Number (BuNo) 09085, seen here, completed its first flight on March 18, 1945.

Initially named the Dauntless II, the aircraft that Heinemann's team formulated at the Washington Statler hotel received the designation XBT2D-1. The Navy considered the R-3350 power plant as the focal component of the design—a fact revealed by Adm. Richardson's remarks at the meeting. To Douglas engineers, however, the key feature of the new aircraft had to be light weight.

As initially presented, the gross weight target was 16,500 pounds. Heinemann set a more demanding goal of only 15,750—750 pounds less than the Navy stipulated. All the aircraft details were examined in the light of the issue of the weight of the components. Instead of overbuilding components to make sure that they would be sufficiently strong, Douglas designers strength-tested the components to ensure that they could satisfy performance requirements while remaining light in weight. Signs reminded the design team that saving 100 pounds of weight would cut takeoff distance by 8 feet, expand the combat radius by 22 miles, raise the rate of climb by 18 feet per minute, and boost speed by 0.3 mph.

When it was ready, the airframe weighed 1,000 pounds less than the target weight. This situation allowed for 1,000 pounds more ordnance on the plane—five times the load of ordnance carried by the SBD. Intended for use as a dive-bomber, the new aircraft required dive brakes. The wing-mounted dive flaps used on the SBD caused inefficiencies in performance and wing design. Accordingly, Douglas employed dive brakes derived from the system designed for the BTD-1, brakes that were mounted on the fuselage rather than the wings. Of the fifteen experimental XBT2D-1 aircraft produced, the first was finished in March 1945, beating the deadline by two weeks. That aircraft made its maiden flight on March 8, 1945.

One of the twenty-five XBT2D-1 prototypes, BuNo 09101, is being subjected to a test flight ca. 1946. The plane was painted overall in Glossy Sea Blue, with white stencils and markings.
National Archives

The XBT2D-1 was armed with a 20 mm cannon in each wing and had hard points under the wings for carrying bombs and rockets. This prototype is armed with a dozen high-velocity aircraft rockets (HVARs) and two Tiny Tim antishipping rockets.
National Archives

Another view of the same XBT2D-1 as shown in the preceding photo illustrates the design of the main landing gear when retracted; the wheels rotated 96 degrees around the axis of the shock strut, in order to fit flat in the landing-gear bays. *National Archives*

For slowing down and stabilizing the BT2D-1 during dive-bombing attacks, the aircraft was equipped with three dive brakes: one on each side of the fuselage and one on the bottom of the fuselage. All of the brakes were just aft of the trailing edges of the wings. All three dive brakes are extended in this photo. *National Archives*

Douglas XBT2D-1, BuNo 09096, was, by April 1946, converted to the prototype of a photoreconnaissance Skyraider and thus was redesignated XBT2D-1P. The teardrop-shaped fairing below the national insignia was for a reconnaissance camera. Further development of a dedicated photoreconnaissance Skyraider was not undertaken.

In addition to the photoreconnaissance prototype, several XBT2D-1s were converted to special-purpose prototypes, including the XBT2D-1N night-fighter, Bu No 09098, with "NATC" markings for the Naval Air Test Center. This version took advantage of the spacious fuselage aft of the cockpit to install two radar-systems operators in side-by-side seats. A small door was provided for them just forward of the national insignia on the right side of the fuselage. The dive brakes were eliminated, and an APS-4 radar pod was mounted under the right wing.

CHAPTER 2
AD-1

The Douglas BT2D-1 Dauntless II went into series production following a Navy order for 548 examples in April 1945, but this order was cut to 277 planes following the defeat of Japan. The Dauntless II was redubbed the Skyraider in February 1946, and the designation BT2D-1 was changed to AD-1 in April 1946. The first flight by an AD-1 was on November 1, 1946. Shown here is AD-1, BuNo 09150, while serving with Carrier Qualification Training Unit 4 (CQTU-4) at NAS Corry Field, Florida, around 1950. New to the production AD-1s was the redesigned carburetor-air scoop to the front of the windscreen. The "252" on the cowling was the side number, an identification number, subject to change, assigned to Navy aircraft.

Flight tests of the first XBT2D-1 yielded impressive results, and on May 5, 1945, the Navy placed an order for 548 production aircraft. The Second World War came to an end before any of the planes could see combat, and then in February 1946, even before any of the aircraft had made a flight, the "Dauntless II" name was replaced by "Skyraider." Then the designation BT2D-1 was dropped two months later and replaced by AD-1.

On November 5, 1946, the first AD-1 took to the air on its maiden flight. It was the first flight of what would in the end total 277 AD-1 aircraft. When the testing disclosed that the aircraft's landing gear needed strengthening, improvements were made that added 400 more pounds to the plane. Worse, the improvements failed to eliminate the difficulty completely.

A new exhaust configuration distinguished the AD-1 from the previous XBT2D-1. The AD-1's exhaust featured two pairs of three exhaust stacks—a change from the XBT2D-1's four stacks on each side of the cowling.

Of the 277 AD-1 aircraft, thirty-five were the first of numerous Skyraider subvariants. These subvariants were the AD-1Q electronic-countermeasures (ECM) aircraft, which had an added second forward-facing seat in the fuselage. There would sit a radio countermeasures operator surrounded by the AN/APR-1 Search Receiver, AN/APA-11 Pulse Analyzer, AN/APA-38 Panoramic Adapter, and MX-356/A Window Dispenser. One accessed this compartment via a door on the fuselage's right side, forward of the dive brake. That access door featured a window, and on the left side of the fuselage there was another corresponding window.

Douglas AD-1, BuNo 09226, was assigned to the US Marine Corps. A good view is available of the wing-fold joint and the six Mk. 9 zero-length rocket launchers, which also doubled as pylons for small bombs, on the outer wing. Two key recognition features found only on the BT2D-1/AD-1 are visible: the flat side of the windshield, and the two small vents just aft of the upper cowl flap; these were carburetor-air bleed vents.

An AD-1 from Attack Squadron 20A (VA-20A), BuNo 09204 and side number 416, cruises over the Bay Area of California on June 2, 1947. The squadron had just begun receiving its AD-1s. The degree of sheen of the Glossy Sea Blue paint is evident in the reflection on the top of the wing. The "B" symbol of Carrier Air Group 19 is on the tail.

The Wright R-3350-24W engine of AD-1, BuNo 09158, is being warmed up preparatory for departure from Naval Air Station (NAS) Floyd Bennett, New York, on June 29, 1947. This Skyraider was assigned to Attack Squadron 3B (VA-3B). Note the arrestor hook under the rudder.

Douglas AD-1 Skyraiders, including one with an APS-4 radar pod under the left wing, are preparing for launching from USS *Coral Sea* (CVB-43) on May 20, 1948. Small horseshoe emblems are on the cowlings.

The part of the national insignia that was on the dive brake of this AD-1 from VA-2B was repeated inside the dive-brake well. The Bureau Number is visible to the far left: 09243.

Atop the fuselage of Douglas AD-1Q, BuNo 09372, aft of the ECM operator's left window, is an air scoop for ventilating his compartment. A snap-on boot called the wing joint cover is installed on the inboard side of the wing-fold joint. A stencil that reads "HANDS OFF" is on the APS-4 radar pod. The white lines on the dorsal fin are sighting marks for the reference of the landing-signal officer (LSO) during the plane's approach for a landing.

By comparison with the AD-1Q in the preceding photo, this example, BuNo 09354, had the ECM operator's ventilation scoop offset to the right side of the fuselage, directly above his door. Also, an antenna mast and a small whip antenna were over the ECM operator's compartment. The object under the right wing is not a radar pod but a dispenser for chaff: strips of metal foil that would be released to confuse enemy radar operators.

As far as is known, this Skyraider is the sole surviving airworthy AD-1. Assigned BuNo 09257, it was restored to flying status by 2007. Currently it is painted to resemble a US Air Force Skyraider of the Vietnam War, operating under the nickname "Bad News" and civil registry number N2AD. *Rich Kolasa*

Smoke billows around "Bad News" as its engine is being warmed up. Details of the tail landing gear, the rudder, and the arrestor hook are visible. *Rich Kolasa*

Pylons have been installed on the wings of "Bad News" and are loaded with SUU-11/A Minigun pods; 500-pound "slick" bombs with standoff fuses, for detonating just aboveground; tube-launched rocket pods; and small bombs.
Rich Kolasa

"Bad News" flies with a full load of ordnance under the wings. Note the curved contours of the exhaust stains aft of the cowling.
Rich Kolasa

An auxiliary fuel tank, or drop tank, without the fins installed is mounted on the centerline hard point of "Bad News." *Rich Kolasa*

The landing gear of "Bad News" is fully lowered during a low pass over the ground. During tests of the AD-1, the main landing gear was found to lack sufficient strength for hard landings on aircraft carrier decks, so measures were taken to strengthen the gear and the wings on the AD-1, which added over 500 pounds to the weight of the aircraft. *Rich Kolasa*

CHAPTER 3
AD-2

The Douglas AD-2 was similar to the AD-1 but with modifications to further strengthen the landing gear and wings. The prototype for the AD-2 was XBT2D-1, BuNo 09108, redesignated XAD-2. Shown here is an AD-1 that was converted to AD-2 standards: BuNo 09195. Two noticeable features that differed from the AD-1 are the elimination of the carburetor-air bleed vents and the redesigned windscreen, with curved sides. The sliding canopy also was revised for the AD-2.

Although improvements had been made over the course of production, the AD-1's landing gear remained inadequate. One aim of the next model of the Skyraider—the AD-2—was to find a solution to that problem. XBT2D-1 Bureau Number (BuNo) 09108 received modifications to turn it into XAD-2.

This aircraft incorporated an improved headrest for the pilot, an antenna behind the revised canopy, and more changes to the exhaust whereby two exhaust stacks now replaced the earlier group of three. In addition, of course, the XAD-2 boasted an improved landing gear.

A new engine was also fitted into the new aircraft. The Wright R-3350-26W power plant, which yielded 2,700 horsepower, was a step up from the AD-1 engine, the R-3350-24, which produced only 2,500 horsepower. Chevrolet, under license from Wright Aeronautical Corporation, manufactured the R-3350-24 at Tonawanda, New York. The boost in horsepower and the light weight of early Skyraiders served to make the AD-2 the fastest variant of the AD ever built, with a maximum speed of 377 miles per hour. Besides speed, the aircraft also had an increased internal fuel capacity of 380 gallons.

In all, fifty-six AD-2 aircraft were produced, in addition to twenty-one AD-2Q electronic-countermeasures airplanes. The ECM version was different from the basic attack aircraft version of the AD-2 in the same way that the AD-1Q was different from the AD-1. The AD-2Q had an electronics suite that comprised an F-27/UPR Wave Trap, AN/APA-11, AN/APA-38, AN/APR-1, AM-40/AIC-4, AN/ASG-10A, AN/APN-1, AN/ARC-1, AN/ARC-5, AN/ARR-2A, and AN/ARQ-2A. One single AD-2Q was adapted to serve as a target tug and accordingly received the new designation AD-2QU.

Douglas AD-2, BuNo 122251, was photographed at NAS Atlantic City, New Jersey, on July 17, 1951. This Skyraider was assigned to Composite Squadron 33 (VC-33). Visible to the rear of the pilot's headrest is the canopy actuator. Also new for the AD-2 was the blade or vane radio antenna aft of the canopy.

Douglas AD-2, BuNo 12225, was assigned to Lt. Cdr. Gerald R. Stablein, of VA-155, and is shown here in a photograph taken around 1949. A white radar pod is mounted under the left wing.

Flaps lowered, AD-2, BuNo 122269 and side number 504, from VA-65, prepares to touch down on the runway at Naval Auxiliary Air Station Santa Rosa, California, in August 1951. Some but not all AD-2s had a static boom on the upper part of the dorsal fin, and that feature is seen here.

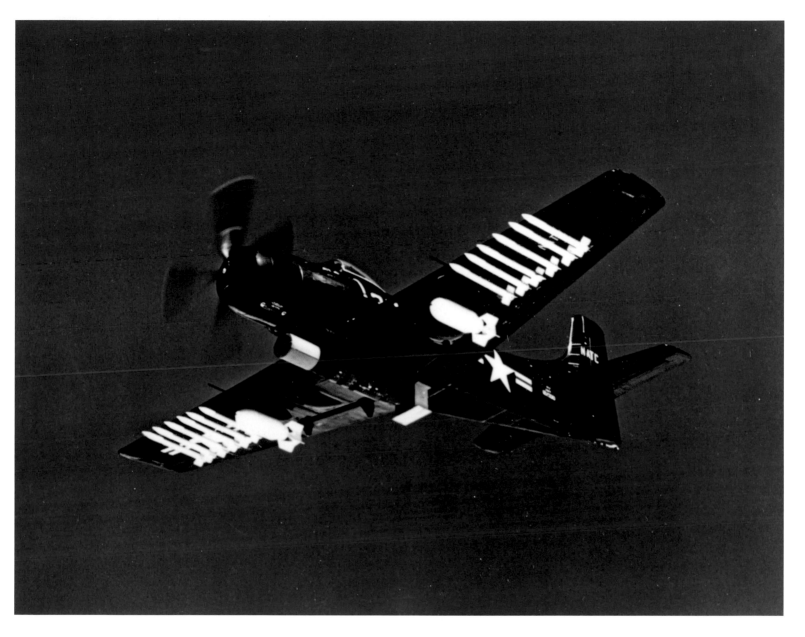

A torpedo is mounted on the centerline, and white bombs and HVARs are installed on the underwing pylons on an AD-2 assigned to the Naval Air Test Center, Patuxent, Maryland, during the 1950s. "NATC" is marked in white on the vertical tail. *Naval History and Heritage Command*

An electronic-countermeasures version of the AD-2 was produced, designated the AD-2Q, with a station inside the fuselage for an ECM operator. A total of twenty-one AD-2Qs were completed; seen here is the first one, BuNo 122366.

The same AD-2Q shown in the preceding photo, BuNo 122366, is seen in markings for VF-152 around 1959 or early 1960, at the airport in San Francisco. The name of the pilot, Ens. W. B. Whitten, is stenciled in white below the side of the windscreen.

One of the AD-2s, BuNo 122226, was selected for conversion to the sole AD-2W early-warning aircraft. The pilot took care of flying the plane and operating the radar equipment, which was housed in the massive radome on the belly. This plane would serve as a model for the AD-3W early-warning aircraft, tasked with detecting and tracking enemy ships or aircraft before they became an imminent threat.

The Douglas AD-2W, BuNo 122226, is observed from the left rear. On April 25, 1951, while serving with VA-65 in Korea, this aircraft was damaged in a midair collision; it landed safely but was damaged beyond repair.

CHAPTER 4

The changes implemented to the landing gear on the AD-2 helped but did not eliminate the difficulties completely. The AD-3 was finally supposed to solve those problems by reinforcing both the main landing gear and the structure of the wing. In addition, the main landing gear's oleo stroke was lengthened to 14 inches. Simultaneously, the landing gear at the rear of the plane was redesigned so that the retracted tailwheel would slightly protrude from the underside of the fuselage.

The canopy shape was modified in subtle ways, as was the bottom of the rudder in most cases. These changes altogether raised the weight of the aircraft by 221 pounds. Due to these changes, in addition to other factors, the top speed of the AD-3 fell by 3 knots, and the service ceiling dropped to 27,000 feet. Just as an electronic-countermeasures version of the earlier models had been produced, so the AD-3Q was manufactured as an electronic-countermeasures version of the AD-3. In all, twenty-three AD-3Q aircraft were made, all of them similar to the ECM variants of the earlier Skyraider versions—other than for the modifications in the airframe itself. It is noteworthy, though, that in addition to the AD-3Q, numerous other subvariants of the AD-3 were also made.

The first three-seat Skyraiders—the AD-3W airborne early warning (AEW) aircraft—were among these other subvariants. In these aircraft, the pilot remained seated in his normal position while the radar operators sat side by side in the voluminous fuselage. A large radome—containing an AN/APS-20 radar antenna—was fitted to the underside of the aircraft. Fuel capacity was expanded to a maximum of 414 gallons, while the three dive brakes and rear landing-gear doors that featured on the standard AD-3 were removed from the AEW model. Auxiliary fins added above and underneath the horizontal stabilizers improved the stability of the aircraft. A total of thirty-one AD-3W planes were manufactured.

Two AD-3E submarine hunter aircraft were later converted from the AD-3W aircraft numbered 122906 and 122907.

Another three-seat version of the AD-3 was the AD-3N night-attack aircraft. The AD-3N's seating configuration was the same as that on the AD-3W, with the rear crew members seated side by side. Also, like the AD-3W, the AD-3N also lacked the dive brakes that featured on standard ADs. Packed with electronics, the night-attack aircraft retained the cannon and attack capability of the main AD-3 planes. Since the AD-3N did not carry the large radome of the -3W, the night-attack version did not need the auxiliary fins.

Designated AD-3S, two submarine killers were made by modifying AD-3N night-attack planes numbers 122910 and 122911. These two AD-3S aircraft were mated with the AD-3E planes to constitute hunter-killer teams.

With the AD-3 model of Skyraiders, Douglas Aircraft finally solved the lingering problem of insufficiently sturdy landing gear, once more redesigning the main gear for greater strength, reinforcing the wings, and installing a new tail gear, whereby the tailwheel retracted only partially into the fuselage. Here, an AD-3 with dive brakes extended is banking away from two other Skyraiders from VA-174, assigned to Carrier Air Group 17, on June 28, 1949. *National Archives*

The same AD-3 seen peeling off from a formation in the preceding photo, side number 410 from VA-174, is viewed from another angle, dive brakes extended, on the same date, June 28, 1949. The pilot was Lt. (j.g.) Farley.

Douglas AD-3, BuNo 122791 and side number 403, is warming its engine at NAS Floyd Bennett, New York, around 1948. At the time, the plane was serving with VA-74. A white APS-4 radome is under the wing. The AD-3s were powered by the Wright R-3350-26W Duplex Cyclone water-injected engine. This AD-3 has the rudder with the straight bottom edge; later in AD-3 production, the design would be noticeably different.

A VA-195 Douglas AD-3, BuNo 122740 and side number 506, is parked at NAS Fallon, Nevada, during September 1949. Note the small, L-shaped pitot tube under the right wing, a few feet from the wingtip.

BuNo 122906, shown here, was one of two AD-3W airborne early-warning Skyraiders converted to AD-3E submarine hunters, in or before 1950, the other being BuNo 122907. These planes, which essentially differed from the airframes they were converted from only in the internal electronic gear, were to perform the antisubmarine search mission, while two AD-3Ns were converted to AD-3S submarine killers. This was part of tests of the efficacy of Skyraider-based submarine hunter-killer teams.

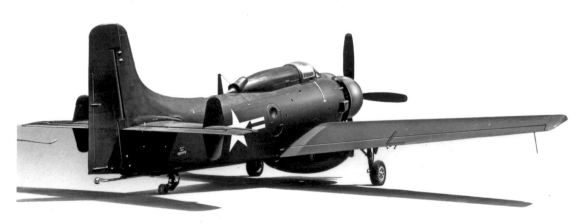

Following the experiments in 1945 with two XBT2D-1s converted to three-seat night-attack aircraft (BuNos 09098 and 09099), no dedicated night-attack Dauntless IIs / Skyraiders were produced until the AD-3N, a three-seat aircraft of which fifteen examples were delivered from fall 1949 to spring 1950. These aircraft also could serve in the radar-countermeasures role. Seen here is the first AD-3N, BuNo 122908.

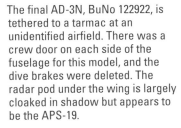

The final AD-3N, BuNo 122922, is tethered to a tarmac at an unidentified airfield. There was a crew door on each side of the fuselage for this model, and the dive brakes were deleted. The radar pod under the wing is largely cloaked in shadow but appears to be the APS-19.

A two-seat ECM version of the AD-3, the AD-3Q, was produced, with twenty-three examples being delivered. A Composite Squadron 33 AD-3Q, BuNo 122875 and side number 49, is seen here, with aerial depth charges and rockets mounted under the wings. *National Archives*

The main instrument panel of an AD-3Q is displayed, with flight instruments on the upper section and armament controls on the lower one. The lower panel was contoured on the bottom to allow space for the pilot's legs.

Although one AD-2, BuNo 122226, had been converted to an AD-2W early-warning aircraft, the first airborne early-warning Skyraider to enter series production was the AD-3W. As seen in a photo of the first AD-3W, BuNo 122877, the plane featured a redesigned canopy, to the rear of which was a turtle deck that enclosed a heating and ventilation system. This plane lacked the vertical fins that would show up on the horizontal stabilizers of subsequent AD-3Ws.

Douglas AD-3W, BuNo 122880, is equipped with fins on the horizontal stabilizers, as seen in a photograph taken March 4, 1949. Two radar operators were stationed in the fuselage aft of the wings, in side-by-side seats. The large, bulbous radome under the belly housed the AS-298/APS-20A radar antenna. The AD-3Ws were not armed with 20 mm cannons.

Douglas AD-3W, BuNo 122879, was assigned to the Naval Air Test Center and is seen in flight carrying two drop tanks on wing pylons.

A Composite Squadron 12 AD-3W numbered 18 is on the tarmac at NAS Quonset Point, Rhode Island, on September 13, 1954. Note the antenna on the top of the dorsal fin.

Radar operators in an AD-3W are conducting preflight checks at NAS Quonset Point on May 3, 1951. Note the radar operators' control panel and indicators.
National Archives

CHAPTER 5
AD-4

The Douglas AD-4 incorporated a number of improvements over the AD-3, including a redesigned windscreen with a larger bulletproof front panel, provisions for carrying the APS-19A radar pod below the right wing, the addition of the P-1 autopilot set, and a change of engine from the R-3350-26W water-injected engine to the R-3350-26WA with water/alcohol injection. Depicted here is an AD-4 from Attack Squadron 115 on June 10, 1950.

Externally, the AD-4 closely resembled its predecessor, the AD-3. Externally, the most obvious difference was the fact that the AD-4 featured a windscreen with a new design and a larger bulletproof panel in the center.

On the inside, however, the AD-4 could be equipped with an APS-19A radar, fitted in a pod located underneath the right wing. This modification necessitated reconfiguring the AD-3 instrument panel and including a P-1 autopilot. In addition, the pilot of the AD-4 was able to wear a G suit.

The AD-4 engine was also a step up from the R-3350-26W. An R-3350-26WA was installed on the AD-4, the "WA" indicating water/alcohol injection in contrast to the water-only injection of the -26W. With the -26WA, water or water/alcohol would be injected for brief periods to inhibit detonation and thereby temporarily boost horsepower. The AD-4's power plant had a military rating of 3,200 horsepower, 500 horsepower more than the rating of the -26W.

As had been the case with previous versions of the plane, there were several subvariants of the AD-4. In addition to the 372 AD-4 aircraft, 165 AD-4B aircraft were manufactured. These planes had four rather than two 20 mm cannon in the wings, and the wings featured a modified Aero 3A bomb rack on the aircraft's center

station, enabling the plane to carry tactical nuclear weapons. These improvements would be retained on all later Skyraider models.

There were other variants too. After the Korean War the AD-4L was created, a version specially adapted for cold weather. Deicing equipment and rubberized black deicing boots were installed along the wing's leading edge. Like the AD-4B, the AD-4L carried four rather than two 20 mm cannons. A total of 63 AD-4L were made.

As had been the case with the earlier versions of the Skyraider, night attack (N), early warning (W), and electronic-countermeasure (Q) versions of the AD-4 were manufactured. In addition, there were seven aircraft that combined the AD-4N and AD-4L features. These planes received the straightforward designation AD-4NL.

In 1951, Great Britain received fifty AD-4W aircraft under the Mutual Defense Assistance Program. Of those planes, fourteen were later transferred to Sweden. In 1959, France was engaged in fighting a nationalist revolution in Algeria. The US supplied Paris a mix of 100 AD-4 and AD-4N aircraft for use in that conflict. Later, in 1962, when French president Charles de Gaulle brought that war to an end by recognizing Algerian independence, the Skyraiders were passed on to the neutralist government of Prince Norodom Sihanouk in Cambodia.

Another AD-4 from VA-115, side number 515, is in flight above water ca. early June 1950.

Lt. Cdr. Levern C. T. Niehaus of VA-105 was the pilot of this AD-4, BuNo 123799 and side number 501, photographed at NAS Cecil Field, Florida, sometime in 1953.

The arrestor hook of a Douglas AD-4B with Lt. Steve Casler of Marine Attack Squadron 324 at the controls has just caught a wire as the plane prepares to land on USS *Saipan* (CVL-48) during a training exercise in support of Marines on Okinawa on February 10, 1954. The AD-4B was a modification of the AD-4, with a strengthened airframe to enable it to carry a tactical nuclear bomb.

An AD-4B assigned to VA-15 and numbered 507 makes a landing on USS *Franklin D. Roosevelt* (CVA-42) during a cruise in the Mediterranean in the last half of 1953. During that deployment, the squadron also flew AD-4s and AD-4Ls (AD-4s modified with cold-weather equipment).

Douglas AD-4, BuNo 123827, is an airworthy Skyraider, currently operating under civil registry number N23827. The plane is marked to replicate an aircraft from VA-195 in the early 1950s. *Rich Kolasa*

Features of the Aeroproducts propeller, the cowling, and the forward fuselage are shown close-up. The two thin, stepped plates jutting from the fuselage just aft of the cowling are glare shields, to protect the pilot's eyes from the glow of the exhausts during night operations. *Rich Kolasa*

On each blade of the Aeroproducts propeller are the "AEROPROP" logo sticker and a yellow stencil with the drawing number (M20A2-162-0), the manufacturer's number (different for each blade), and "LOW ANGLE 28.2" and "HIGH ANGLE 69.2." *Rich Kolasa*

The squadron insignia of VA-195 at the time of the Korean War is affixed to the fuselage below the windscreen. A static boom is attached to the top of the dorsal fin—a feature sometimes observed in vintage photos of AD-4s, and an L-shaped pitot tube with a red cover over it is under the right wing. *Rich Kolasa*

Douglas AD-4, BuNo 123827 and civil registry number N23827, is viewed from the right rear with the engine running. Note the notched bottom of the rudder, a feature introduced during AD-3 production. *Rich Kolasa*

The AD-4 has just lifted off the ground, and the landing gear is in the process of retracting. Note how the tail gear retracted forward. *Rich Kolasa*

Douglas AD-4, BuNo 123827, flies low over the ground with the cockpit canopy closed. On this occasion, no underwing stores were carried on the pylons. *Rich Kolasa*

The same Skyraider demonstrates its dive brakes during a low-level pass. *Rich Kolasa*

Flaps and landing gear lowered, the AD-4 descends for a landing. The AD-4's landing gear was once again strengthened during production, in a seemingly nonstop effort to enable the plane to withstand rough landings on aircraft carriers. *Rich Kolasa*

Douglas AD-4, BuNo 123827, is observed in an indoor setting with its wings folded, showing details of the engine, propeller, left main landing-gear doors, and drop tanks. *David Doyle*

The engine is depicted. The Wright R-3350-26WA Duplex Cyclone 18-cylinder air-cooled radial engine of the AD-4 was rated at 2,700 horsepower on takeoff and 2,100 horsepower at 14,500 feet. *David Doyle*

With the wings folded, the width of the AD-4 was reduced from 50 feet, ¼ inch to 23 feet, 10½ inches, saving considerable deck space; while the height was only increased from 15 feet, 8¼ inches to 16 feet, 7⅝ inches. *David Doyle*

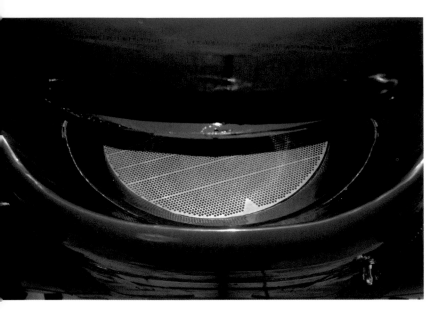

On the bottom of the fuselage aft of the cowling is the air scoop for the oil cooler, part of which is visible inside the opening. *David Doyle*

On the left side of the Skyraiders, starting with the AD-2, there were only two upper exhausts, and three in the lower position. *David Doyle*

As seen from the right, the cowling consists of a fixed nose section, a removable antidrag ring, and the cowl flaps, which are in the open position. On the right side of the plane are six exhaust stubs, in two groups of three each. *David Doyle*

The outboard side of the right main landing gear, including the tire and the wheel, is displayed, along with the forward landing-gear door, to the front of the shock strut. *David Doyle*

The shock strut of the left main landing gear is viewed from the inboard side. Affixed to the strut is a data plate and placard with instructions that includes a graph on proper inflation and maintenance of the strut. Also shown is the left disc brake. *David Doyle*

In a photo taken under the left main-gear well, to the front are the shock strut and the forward landing-gear-bay door. Attached to the shock is the triangular gear-actuating linkage. To the right is the inboard gear-bay door. *David Doyle*

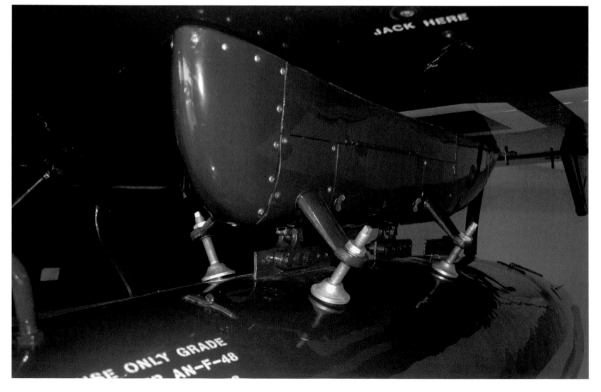

The left pylon is shown with a drop tank shackled to it. Jutting from the bottom of the pylon are four sway braces, which are adjustable and serve to tighten the connection of the drop tank or bomb to the pylon. On the side of the pylon is an access door with a piano hinge at the top and two wing-type fasteners near the bottom. *David Doyle*

On the inboard section of the right wing-fold joint is a boot, which snaps in place and protects the items inside the wing, including the cannon, from the elements. Jutting from the upper part of the inboard wing joint is a wing-locking lug. *David Doyle*

In a view of the right side of the fuselage and wing, a recessed handgrip is below the cockpit canopy, and a step with a sprung door is at the bottom of the white stripe below the canopy. In the foreground, the forward end of the dive brake is in view. *David Doyle*

On the left side of the fuselage are three recessed handholds, with stencils that read "HAND GRIP" immediately below them. *David Doyle*

The tail landing gear is viewed from the right side. The tire is the solid-rubber type used for aircraft carrier operations; there was a pneumatic tire available for use when the planes were based on land. *David Doyle*

The right side of the tail of AD-4, BuNo 123827, is displayed, including the static boom on the upper front of the dorsal fin, static dischargers on the upper trailing edge of the rudder, the rudder trim tabs, and the arrestor hook. On the tail of the fuselage are access panels for empennage and rudder mechanisms. *David Doyle*

For operations in very cold climates, the Douglas AD-4L was developed, with a total of sixty-three being delivered. This winterized Skyraider featured deicer boots on the leading edges of the wings, dorsal fin, and horizontal stabilizers. Whereas the basic AD-4 had one 20 mm cannon in each wing, inboard of the wing joint, the AD-4L had a 20 mm cannon in that position in addition to a second one in the outer wing section. Depicted here is BuNo 127852.

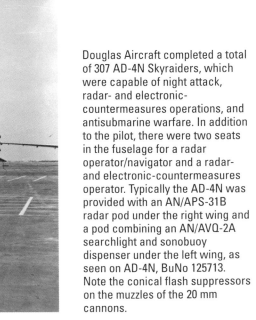

Douglas Aircraft completed a total of 307 AD-4N Skyraiders, which were capable of night attack, radar- and electronic-countermeasures operations, and antisubmarine warfare. In addition to the pilot, there were two seats in the fuselage for a radar operator/navigator and a radar- and electronic-countermeasures operator. Typically the AD-4N was provided with an AN/APS-31B radar pod under the right wing and a pod combining an AN/AVQ-2A searchlight and sonobuoy dispenser under the left wing, as seen on AD-4N, BuNo 125713. Note the conical flash suppressors on the muzzles of the 20 mm cannons.

During the Korean War, a total of 100 AD-4N night-attack Skyraiders were converted to AD-4NAs, which had the night-attack and antisubmarine-warfare electronics removed to allow the aircraft to transport heavier payloads. This AD-4NA, BuNo 124134, was assigned to the Fleet Airborne Electronics Training Atlantic in 1953.

Douglas AD-4NA, BuNo 126957 and side number 154, was assigned to the Naval Air Reserve Unit at Glenview, Illinois, and was photographed on July 30, 1955. The oval window on the crew door on the fuselage was a blister type, not flat.

The AD-4NL was a winterized version of the AD-4N, of which thirty-seven were converted. This example, BuNo 124745 and side number 04, was assigned to VC-35 and is seen during a mission on October 6, 1951, with the searchlight pod under the left wing.

An AN/APS-31B radar pod is under the right wing of Douglas AD-4NL, BuNo 124730, from VC-35, based on USS *Essex*. The plane, with its arrestor hook lowered, is flying low over the ocean off Korea during the war on that peninsula, in 1951 or 1952.

The Douglas AD-4Q fulfilled the radar-countermeasures and attack roles; a total of thirty-nine were completed. Illustrated here is an AD-4Q numbered 519, loaded with three 1,000-pound general-purpose bombs and a dozen HVARs. Note the ECM operator's window on the fuselage, above the left 20 mm cannon barrel, and the air scoop for the ECM operator's compartment to the front of the vane antenna atop the fuselage.

Representing VA-25 was AD-4Q, BuNo 124045 and side number 519, photographed at a foggy airfield ca. mid-1950. The bubble-shaped window of the ECM operator is clearly visible on the aft fuselage.

This Douglas AD-4Q, BuNo 124046, immediately followed the AD-4Q in the preceding photo (124045) on the assembly line. This Skyraider is parked at NAS Atlantic City, New Jersey, on July 17, 1951, while assigned to VC-33.

The AD-4W was similar in design to the AD-3W airborne early-warning Skyraider. Douglas completed 158 examples. These planes featured an AN/APS-20A S-band search radar, with a large radome on the belly for the antenna. Two new features were on the wings: fixed leading-edge slats on the outer wing sections, for better performance at low speeds, and a small spoiler on the leading-edge center-wing section, but on the right side only. As seen on this example, BuNo 124761, the AD-4W had round main-gear wheel wells and no side gear-bay doors; this also was true for the AD-3Ws.

Douglas AD-4W, BuNo 124099, was photographed at the airport at El Segundo, California, in 1951. Note the rod-shaped brace from the radome to the bottom of the wing, visible to the front of the left main landing-gear strut.

With the AD-5 variant, the Skyraider underwent some significant changes, in contrast to the rather minor differences between earlier versions of the plane. The AD-5 had the same armament as the AD-4B, but its fuselage and canopy were much larger than the earlier model, with 9 inches added to the width of the fuselage at its center. The canopy was made larger so that the pilot and an observer could sit side by side at the front. In US Navy versions of the AD-5, only the pilot was provided with flight controls. When the AD-5 was adopted by the US Air Force and later by the South Vietnamese air force, a second set of flight controls were added to the observer seat. Toward the rear of the cockpit, the canopy was also expanded to accommodate expanded seating for as many as two more crewmen, though some variants only had seating for one crewman in that position.

The AD-5 fuselage was also slightly lengthened—a modification that entailed shifting the power plant forward by 8 inches. The vertical tail was also enlarged by 50 percent. Although all these changes were fairly significant, the resultant weight increase was only 581 pounds over the empty weight of the AD-4—bringing the AD-5 empty weight to 12,874 pounds.

The first AD-5, an experimental model converted from AD-4 124006, took off on its maiden flight on August 17, 1951. A few slight modifications later and the AD-5 began regular production.

A total of 212 of the AD-5s were built, and in addition 239 AD-5N night-attack subvariants were made. These aircraft were crewed by three men—a pilot, an ECM operator to his right, and a radar operator behind the pilot.

AD-5, BuNo 132479, was turned into an antisubmarine AD-5S aircraft with a three-man crew. This one-off plane flew with VX-1 squadron based at Naval Air Station Key West.

Another wide-bodied variation of the Skyraider was the ECM-adapted AD-5Q. This variant traced its origins to a prototype modified from the final AD-5N, BuNo 135054, which first took to the air as an AD-5Q in October 1956. Four men crewed each of the fifty-four AD-5Q aircraft—the pilot and navigator up front and two ECM operators to the rear.

The AD-5W, the airborne early-warning version of the AD-5, had a crew of three—pilot and navigator in the front position, with the radar operator behind the pilot, underneath a canopy covered in metal. In all, 218 production models of the AD-5W were manufactured.

In 1962, the Tri-Service aircraft designation system was introduced, and the AD-5 was renamed A-1E. The AD-5W became the EA-1E, the AD-5Q was renamed the EA-1F, and the AD-5N was redesignated the A-1G.

Originally conceived as a submarine hunter-killer aircraft, the Douglas AD-5 entered production as a daytime attack plane. It took the basic Skyraider airframe and installed side-by-side seats in the cockpit for the pilot and the assistant pilot or observer, who was not equipped with flight controls. (Later, the US Air Force would operate this aircraft, installing flight controls for a copilot in the right seat.) To achieve this cockpit arrangement, the fuselage was redesigned, including a widened area in the midsection to accommodate the new cockpit and rear cabin. The canopy extended aft, over cabin space for two more crewmen aft of the cockpit. The vertical tail was increased in size. Two 20 mm cannons were installed in each wing.

On the tarmac at Naval Auxiliary Air Station Brown Field, San Diego, California, on November 4, 1958, are two Skyraiders, including, in the foreground, AD-5, BuNo 132644, with markings for Aviation Fleet Marine Force Pacific on the fuselage. This AD-5 was based at that time at Marine Corps Air Station (MCAS) El Toro, California. The inboard pylons were the Mk. 51, all new for the AD-5, with a straight, slanted front edge; these were capable of carrying 2,300 pounds of ordnance or fuel tanks.

This Skyraider, BuNo 135178 and civil registry number N62466, was an AD-5W early-warning plane that was restored to resemble an AD-5. It is maintained in flying condition by a private owner. The aircraft is seen from the front with wings folded and 5-inch HVARs mounted on the launchers. *David Doyle*

The AD-5 is viewed from the left front, showing the slab-sided design of the fuselage alongside the cockpit. The engine of the AD-5 was mounted 8 inches farther forward than on preceding models of Skyraiders. *David Doyle*

Douglas AD-5, BuNo 135178, bears reproduction markings for Marine Attack Squadron 322 (VMA-322) "Polkadots," complete with the squadron's white wingtip and fin tip with red polka dots. *David Doyle*

The left wing-fold joint is viewed close-up. This plane lacks the 20 mm cannons. The red object protruding from the leading edge of the center wing section is the wing locking-pin flag, nicknamed the "beer can." It was a visual indicator of when the wing was not locked. *David Doyle*

Specifications			
	AD-1	**AD-5 (A-1E)**	**A-1H**
Wingspan:	50 feet, ¼ inch	50 feet, ¼ inch	50 feet, ¼ inch
Length	38 feet, 10 inch	40 feet, 1 inch	38 feet, 10 inch
Height	15 feet, 8¼ inches	15 feet, 11 inches	15 feet, 8¼ inches
Empty weight	10,987 pounds	12,300 pounds	11,968 pounds
Power plant	Wright R-3350-24W 18-cylinder air-cooled radial engine	Wright R-3350-26WA 18-cylinder air-cooled radial engine	Wright R-3350-26WA 18-cylinder air-cooled radial engine
Horsepower:	2,500	2,700	2,700
Armament	2 × 20 mm M3 cannons	4 × 20 mm M3 cannons	4 × 20 mm M3 cannons
Ammunition	200 rounds per gun	200 rounds per gun	200 rounds per gun
Bombload	8,000 lbs. max.	8,000 lbs. max.	8,000 lbs. max.
Maximum speed	366 mph	311 mph	322 mph
Service ceiling	33,000 feet	26,000 feet	28,500 feet
Range	1,940	1,202 miles	1,316 miles
Crew	1	2	1

The left side of the cowling, the cockpit area of the fuselage, and the windscreen and canopy are displayed. Note the windshield wiper. *David Doyle*

The cockpit canopy is in the open position. Note the quilted insulation material on the aft bulkhead of the cockpit. The red knob below the rear of the windscreen is the exterior canopy control. *David Doyle*

In a left-rear view of AD-5, BuNo 135178, the fairing on top of the aft fuselage to the immediate front of the dorsal fin is for the AN/ARN-6 radio-compass antenna. On the upper front of the dorsal fin is a beacon and a static boom.
David Doyle

The AD-5 had only the forward fairings for the main landing gear, mounted to the fronts of the shock struts. The canopy over the rear cabin is tinted dark blue.
David Doyle

Under the tri-service aircraft designation system initiated in 1962, the Douglas AD-5 was redesignated A-1E when employed as an attack aircraft and UA-1E when used as a utility plane. The National Museum of the US Air Force, at Dayton, Ohio, preserves a Douglas A-1E, serial number 52-132649. On March 1, 1966, Maj. Bernard Fisher, while flying this plane, rescued another pilot who had been shot down over South Vietnam. For this deed, Fisher was awarded the Medal of Honor. Subsequently, after being damaged in combat, this Skyraider was transferred to the museum in 1968. Note the solid-steel main wheels, which, on many USAF Skyraiders, replaced the always-problematic spoked wheels.
National Museum of the United States Air Force

Douglas A-1E, serial number 52-132649, is seen in its indoor display space at the National Museum of the US Air Force, with a collection of bombs, air-to-ground rocket launchers, and Minigun pods on the pylons. The plane is finished in the light gray over white camouflage initially used for USAF A-1Es. *David Doyle*

A section of black paint was applied to each side of the fuselage on some gray-over-white Skyraiders to mask engine exhaust stains. Note the lack of dive brakes on the AD-5/A-1E. *David Doyle*

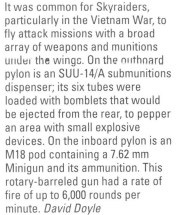

It was common for Skyraiders, particularly in the Vietnam War, to fly attack missions with a broad array of weapons and munitions under the wings. On the outboard pylon is an SUU-14/A submunitions dispenser; its six tubes were loaded with bomblets that would be ejected from the rear, to pepper an area with small explosive devices. On the inboard pylon is an M18 pod containing a 7.62 mm Minigun and its ammunition. This rotary-barreled gun had a rate of fire of up to 6,000 rounds per minute. *David Doyle*

Weapons under the left wing of the A-1E are viewed from the rear. A bare-metal napalm bomb is to the right, just outboard of the Minigun pod. *David Doyle*

A dramatic wide-angle photograph encompasses the forward cockpit of the A-1E at the National Museum of the US Air Force. Unlike the Navy version of this aircraft, the Air Force version had flight controls, including a stick and rudder pedals, for the right-seat man. A gunsight is mounted over the pilot's instrument panel. *National Museum of the United States Air Force*

CHAPTER 7
AD-6 (A-1H)

The Douglas AD-6 (redesignated A-1H in 1962) was a single-seat attack aircraft that was, in effect, an improved version of the Douglas AD-4B, retaining that earlier model's ability to deliver tactical nuclear weapons. The fuselage was strengthened to allow the carriage of a 3,500-pound payload on the centerline hard point, while the inboard pylons were rated for 3,000 pounds each. Photographed at NAS Cecil Field, Florida, on June 9, 1954, is one of the 713 AD-6s completed, BuNo 135236, from VA-15.

Before the AD-5, all the special multiseat subvariant Skyraiders derived from the main single-seat version. Thus the AD-1Q was a derivative of the AD-1. Starting with the introduction of the AD-5, however, the single-seat attack plane lost its centrality and was relegated to having its own number, the AD-6, such as subversions previously carried.

Featuring a beefed-up center section, the AD-6 was an improvement over the AD-4B. It could carry a centerline payload of 3,500 pounds, and its inner-wing racks were rated to 3,000 pounds each. Like most Skyraiders, the AD-6 also had fuselage-mounted dive brakes, a feature that had been absent on the AD-5.

Another new feature of the AD-6 was bolted-on armor that protected the pilot and vital components. This armor, which could be removed, was an advantage when the aircraft played its ground-attack role. The plane's electronics were simplified as compared

with those on the earlier AD-4, a measure aimed at compensating for extra weight acquired with the armor.

Despite that measure, the empty weight of the aircraft rose by 300 pounds and speed fell from 325 to 285 knots. The aircraft's canopy was modified to make it jettisonable.

First flown in June 1953, the AD-6 was produced in a total of 713 units, with the last delivery received in August 1956. The name of the AD-6, like other Skyraiders still in service, was redesignated, becoming the A-1H in September 1962.

The AD-6 aircraft with BuNos 142010 through 142081—the last of the planes to be produced—were fitted out to accommodate the Douglas D-704 buddy system refueling pod. Following service bulletins AD/SC 606 and 661, earlier AD-6 aircraft were also modified while in service to accommodate that refueling pod.

A Douglas AD-6 flies a mission over a body of water ca. 1954. At the time, the plane was attached to VA-85. Only the last four numbers of its Bureau Number are visible: 4605, so the full BuNo was 134605.

Douglas A-1H, BuNo 139606, survives in flying condition and features a mixed bag of Vietnam War markings, including the well-known bumblebee tail art of Skyraiders from VA-176 while deployed with USS *Intrepid*, and the "AH" tail code and green-arrow tail symbol worn by planes of VA-165 while assigned to USS *Oriskany*. The plane currently flies under civil registry number NX39606. *Rich Kolasa*

Flaps lowered, A-1H, BuNo 139696, comes in for a landing. After the omission of the dive brakes on the AD-5/A1-E, this feature was restored on the AD-6/A-1H. *Rich Kolasa*

During a takeoff, the main-gear wheels are rotating as the struts swing up toward the wings, and the tail gear is retracting in a forward arc. *Rich Kolasa*

The A-1H was equipped with the side landing-gear doors, which, along with the forward landing-gear doors, formed a bulge under each wing when the gear was retracted, as seen in this photo. *Rich Kolasa*

In this photo of A-1H, BuNo 139696, the side doors of the main landing gear are partly open. The tailwheel protruded slightly below the bottom of the fuselage when retracted. *Rich Kolasa*

The National Naval Aviation Museum in Pensacola, Florida, preserves Douglas A-1H, BuNo 135300, on static display. Douglas delivered this Skyraider to the Navy on June 29, 1954. It saw combat in the Vietnam War from 1965 to 1968 with, successively, VA-25, operating from USS *Midway* (CV-41); VA-52 aboard USS *Ticonderoga* (CVA-14); and once again with VA-25, this time aboard USS *Coral Sea* (CVA-43). This Skyraider was retired from the service on April 10, 1968, and has been on display at the National Naval Aviation Museum since 1975. The plane bears markings for VA-25. *Rich Kolasa*

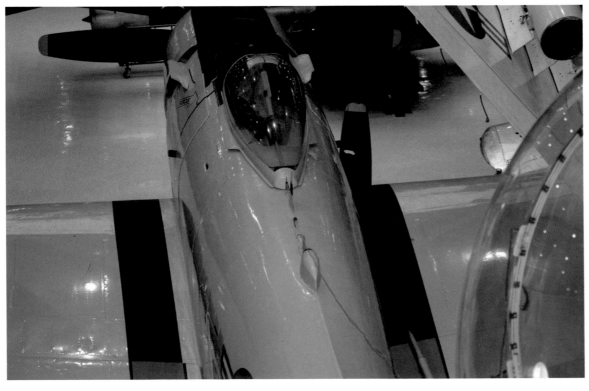

The fuselage and center wing section of A-1H, BuNo 135300, are viewed from above, including the canopy, the nonslip panels on the wings, and the fairing on the top of the fuselage for the loop antenna. *David Doyle*

The empennage is viewed from above. All of the control surfaces of the Skyraiders, including the rudder and the elevators, were clad with aluminum-alloy skin. *David Doyle*

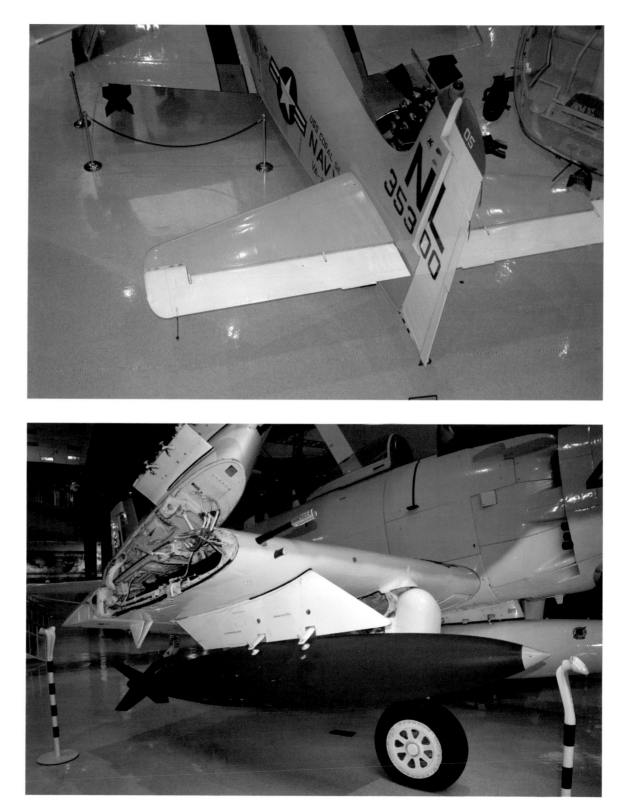

Details of the right inboard pylon and the wing-fold joint are in view. Note the wing locking-pin flag, or "beer can," jutting from the leading edge of the center wing section below the cannon barrel. *David Doyle*

Bombs and a rocket pod are mounted on the pylons on the right folded wing. Note the 20 mm spent-casing port on the bottom of the wing, between the two pylons to the right. *David Doyle*

The same bombs and rocket pod are observed from the rear. *David Doyle*

The rocket pod is viewed from a closer perspective from the rear. This pod carried nineteen 2.75-inch folding-fin rockets. *David Doyle*

A view of the munitions mounted on the wing pylons of A-1H, BuNo 135300, also includes details of the right aileron, the aileron trim tab, and the rear hinge for the folding wing. *David Doyle*

The dive brake on the right side of the fuselage is displayed, showing the recesses in the skin of the fuselage for the two hinges on the forward edge of the brake. Three recessed handgrips are on the fuselage, forward of the dive brake. *David Doyle*

The arrestor hook, the bottom of the rudder, and the tail landing gear are seen from the right side facing forward. The shaft of the arrestor hook was typically painted in 4-inch black and white bands, for ready visibility for deck crewmen. *David Doyle*

In a view of the vertical tail from the left side, a beacon with a red dome is at the top of the dorsal fin, with a static boom below it. Above the "N" in the tail code are two teardrop-shaped identification lights; the upper one has a red lens, and the lower one a clear lens. *David Doyle*

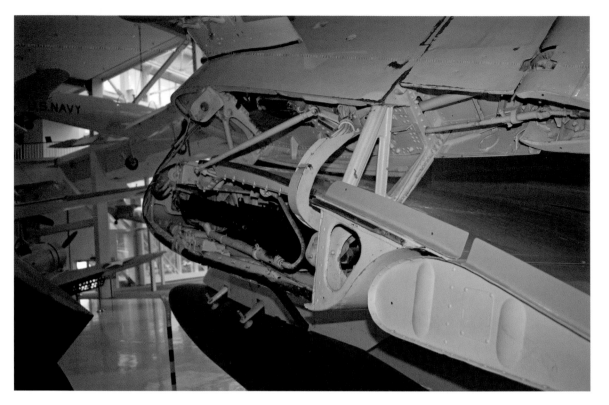

The left wing-fold joint is shown. With the cover removed from the joint, the receiver of the 20 mm cannon is visible inside the center wing section. In the foreground is the outer end of the left flap. The diagonal rod between the folded, outer wing and the center wing section is the aileron push-pull tube. *David Doyle*

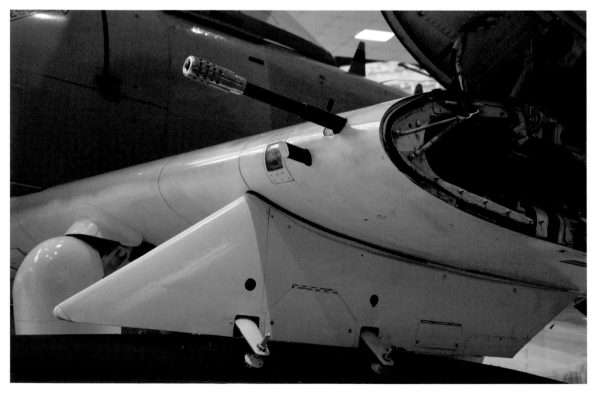

A photo of the left inboard pylon and its two left sway braces also provides details of the wing locking-pin flag, 20 mm cannon barrel, and a clear, square lens for an approach light. *David Doyle*

During the latter part of AD-4 production, external armor was installed on the sides and bottom of the fuselage, between the cowling and the cockpit. This was in the form of shape-fitting panels. The installation of add-on armor continued in later models of Skyraiders, and the armor plates on the left side of A-1H, BuNo 135300, are seen here. Note how the small plate to the front of the wing is cut to fit around the leading edge of the wing. *David Doyle*

Beginning with AD-4 production, nose flaps became available for Skyraiders. These consisted of a disc that was fitted between the propeller and the front of the engine, and hinged flaps or baffles around the inside of the front of the cowling. The flaps were deployed for operations in cold weather, to prevent the engine from becoming too cold. *David Doyle*

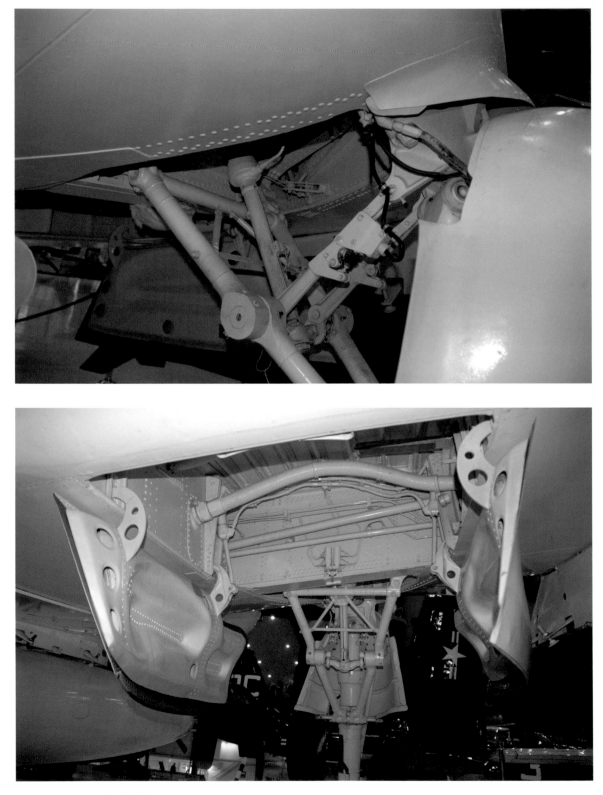

The upper part of the left main landing gear is seen from the outboard side. To the right is the front fairing; note the matching piece of fairing attached to the wing at the upper right. Also in view are the actuating links to the rear of the shock strut, and the left outboard landing-gear door.

In a photo of the right main landing gear and its bay, the front fairing is forward of the shock strut, and on each side of the bay is a bay door, each of which has two hinges and a contoured inner skin for additional strength. *David Doyle*

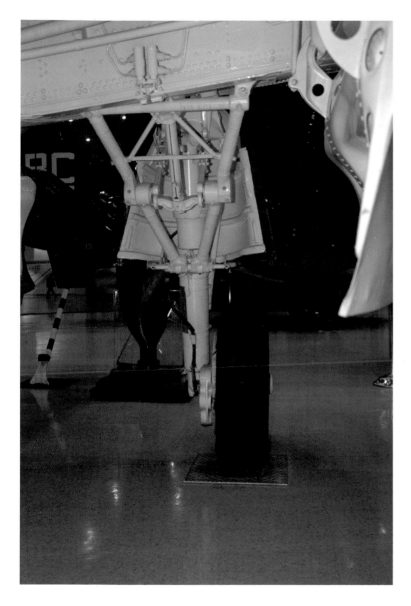

The lower part of the right main landing gear, including the tire, is seen from dead astern. Between the bottom of the shock strut and the tire is part of the brake assembly. *David Doyle*

The left main landing-gear bay is viewed facing aft. Liberal use was made of hat-channel stiffeners arranged fore and aft on the top of the bay for extra structural strength. *David Doyle*

CHAPTER 8
AD-7 (A-1J)

The final model of the Skyraider was the AD-7, redesignated A-1J in 1962. It chiefly varied from the AD-6/A-1H by having further strengthening of the landing gear, the wings, and the engine mount. Also, the Wright R-3350-26WA engine of the AD-6 was replaced by the Wright R-3350-26WB. Shown here in Gull Gray over White camouflage is AD-7, BuNo 142081, assigned to VA-215.

The AD-7—later redesignated the A-1J—was the last development of the Douglas Skyraider. An important feature of the AD-7 was its Wright R-3350-26WB power plant, an engine that offered higher speed and increased payload-carrying capacity. This engine, however, required strengthened engine mounts.

To cope with the increase in power, the landing gear and outer wing spars were strengthened, as compared with those features on the AD-6. Because of these upgrades, the AD-7 could carry two 400-gallon drop tanks on the inner wing pylons. Thus the AD-7s were able to carry the Douglas D-704 "Buddy Store," an external, hose-and-drogue refueling system that boasted low drag. This system enabled the Skyraider to fuel up any other aircraft that was fitted out with a receptor. Additionally, a few of the AD-6 Skyraiders were also adapted to use this system.

The AD-7 was the most combat-capable Skyraider, due to the aircraft incorporating lessons learned by the US Navy and Douglas Aircraft over the course of prior production. Nevertheless, after initially ordering 240 AD-7s, the Navy later brought production to a close after only seventy-two airplanes had been manufactured.

When AD-7 BuNo 142081 rolled off the Douglas assembly line on February 18, 1957, it was the last of 3,180 Skyraiders produced. There were some proposals made during the 1960s that Douglas might tool up to resume manufacture of the Skyraider; these ideas never reached fruition, and BuNo 142081 thus remained the last of the Skyraiders. This specific plane was flying with VA-52 when it was downed by antiaircraft fire near Phú Cường, 10 miles north of Saigon, in Gia Định Province, South Vietnam, on January 3, 1966.

Outside a hangar at NAS Moffett Field, California, on July 20, 1963, is A-1J, BuNo 142034, with markings for VA-165, based at that time on USS *Oriskany* (CVA-34). The arrow symbols on the tail and the fuselage were green. The "AH" tail code pertained to Carrier Air Group 16.

A total of seventy-two AD-7s were completed; this example was the fifth one built, BuNo 142014, and it is shown parked at Marine Corps Auxiliary Air Station Yuma, Arizona, on December 3, 1959, while assigned to VA-115.

An AD-7 Skyraider is nearing completion on the Douglas Aircraft assembly line at El Segundo, California, on January 22, 1957. This airframe was the final Skyraider ever completed: construction number 11561 and USN BuNo 142081.

This A-1J, BuNo 142036, assigned to VA-196, was piloted by Cdr. James A. Donovan, who took over command of the squadron after returning from its final combat deployment to Vietnam with Skyraiders. Under his command, VA-196 transitioned to the A-6A Intruder. The photo was taken in early 1966 and shows Commander Donovan in the pilot's seat.

CHAPTER 9
Skyraider in Combat

A Douglas AD-2, side number 406, from VA-154 is poised on the flight deck of USS *Antietam* (CV-36) during 1948. Attack Squadron 154 received a dozen AD-2s in August 1948.

Originally envisioned as a powerful carrier-based attack aircraft that was also suitable as a scouting platform, the Skyraider proved its capability in those roles during its service in the Korean War. For ground attack, the US Air Force in Korea relied on the F-51 Mustang. Back during the Second World War, the F-51 had been a powerful air-superiority fighter. Used for ground attack in Korea, however, the Mustang, with its liquid-cooled engine, was vulnerable to ground fire and was ill suited its job. The new jet aircraft operated by the Air Force were also badly suited for the ground-attack role in that conflict. These issues recurred when the United States became engaged in the war in Vietnam.

In 1949, the US Air Force evaluated the Skyraider but pursued an ever-widening spectrum of jet aircraft instead. In 1963, the Air Force was compelled to accept the apparently dated Skyraider when the Navy resolved to hand over two squadrons of A-1E/G aircraft to South Vietnam. Since the Air Force was tasked with training the Vietnamese on these and other aircraft, it was the Air Force's lot to deal with the Skyraider. The specific unit that took on the training task was the 1st Air Commando Wing at Hurlburt Field, Florida.

During the conflict in Indochina, US Navy Skyraiders took off from aircraft carriers to perform the many varied tasks—other than nuclear weapons delivery—for which the aircraft were designed.

More and more Skyraiders were passed on to the South Vietnamese and to the US Air Force, which had become familiar with the difficulties of using jet fighters as attack aircraft in Vietnam.

Inevitably, however, the Navy accepted the idea of a fleet of combat aircraft that were all jet powered. The last US Navy Skyraider to take to the air flew from the deck of the USS *John F. Kennedy* on December 20, 1969. The US Air Force flew its last A-1 in combat over Vietnam on November 7, 1972.

In the foreground on the flight deck of the carrier USS *Leyte* (CV-32) on May 4, 1948, are two Douglas AD-2s from Attack Squadron 34 (VA-34). The Skyraider in the foreground has aerial torpedoes mounted on the centerline and wing racks. Under the outer-wing sections are HVARs. In the background are TBF/TBM Avenger torpedo bombers.

A Composite Squadron 35 (VC-35) AD-1Q ECM Skyraider is parked at an unidentified base ca. 1949. A white APS-4 radar pod is under the wing, and a white-colored, teardrop-shaped fairing for ECM equipment is below the "VC-35" marking on the fuselage.

Douglas AD-3 number 512 from VA-195 is viewed from the cockpit of another Skyraider during a flight in January 1950 while assigned to USS *Boxer* (CV-21). This plane probably was the same AD-3 number 512 and tail code B, BuNo 122750, that was flown by Ens. Robert Bennett of VA-195 during 1950. The tip of the vertical tail was green.

Another VA-195 AD-3, number 514, is in flight over the Western Pacific in January 1950. On the right pylon is a practice-bomb dispenser, which carried small bombs that were ballistically similar to the full-sized bombs and were used to save the expense of expending the real things.

Aviation ordnancemen on the flight deck of USS *Philippine Sea* are wheeling fragmentation bombs around the front of an AD-4, side number 503, from VA-116 during operations off the coast of Korea on October 19, 1950. *National Archives*

Loaded with bombs, AD-4, BuNo 123830, of VA-115 is about to depart on a strike mission from USS *Philippine Sea* (CV-47) against Communist forces in Korea on October 19, 1950. The wing is being lowered on the Skyraider to the left. *National Archives*

Although Skyraiders came along too late to see combat in World War II, they were prominent players in the Korean war of 1950–53. Here, an AD-3 is visible a little above the center of the photo, recovering from a dive in which it released a 2,000-pound bomb on one of two adjacent bridges over the Yalu River at Sinuiju on November 15, 1950. This was in a concentrated attempt to cut off Chinese supply lines to communist forces in Korea. A full complement of the frag bombs are mounted under the left wing. *National Archives*

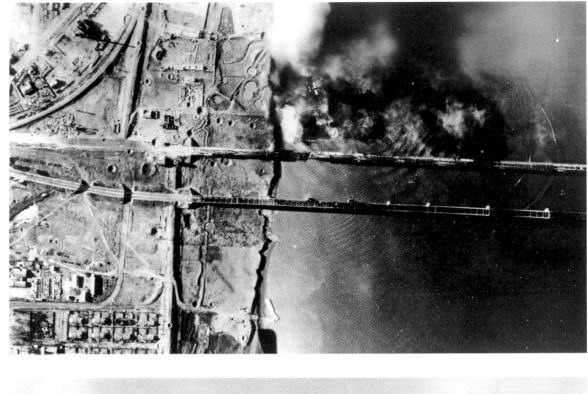

A Douglas AD-3 airborne early-warning (AEW) Skyraider from VC-11 makes a pass, arrestor hook lowered, alongside USS *Leyte* (CV-36) in waters off Korea in August 1951. Side number 32 is on the cowling, and the tail code is ND.

During an airstrike by planes from Task Force 77 on a North Korean railroad line near the Sea of Japan in October 1951, a Skyraider is viewed from its rear as it enters its bombing run over two bombed-out bridges. Much of the span to the right has been destroyed, and the Skyraider appears to be trying for more destruction to that bridge.

Douglas AD-3, BuNo 122805, suffered irreparable damage after a Douglas AD-4Q crashed into it on the flight deck of USS *Leyte* on January 14, 1952. Deck crewmen are hustling to clear the wreckage so that flight operations can resume.

A ground crewman, *left*, is waving the pilot of Douglas AD-4NA, BuNo 125750 and side number 411, into position on a dirt airstrip on Yon Don, a United Nations–occupied island in Wonsan Harbor, North Korea, in May 1953. The Skyraider was assigned to Fighter Squadron 54 (VF-54) and had a letter *S* on the vertical tail. *National Archives*

At least twenty-one Skyraiders are undergoing construction at Douglas Aircraft. The first and third airframes are airborne early-warning planes, either AD-3Ws or AD-4Ws. The remainder are single-seat attack aircraft, likely AD-3s or AD-4s. Most of the planes have the windscreens installed, but only the closest five have the sliding canopies installed. *National Museum of the United States Air Force*

By the time this photo of AD-6 Skyraiders from VA-42 aboard USS *Forrestal* (CV-59) was taken on March 14, 1956, over a year had passed since the Navy issued a directive that Light Gull Gray over Insignia White camouflage replace Glossy Sea Blue on carrier aircraft. Nevertheless, at this point there was still a mix of the old blue and new gray-and-white camouflage on the Skyraiders. Number 401 was the aircraft of Lt. L. W. Squires. Note the sawtooth-style upper edge of the area of black paint applied to the side of the fuselage of that plane, an early attempt at masking the heavy exhaust staining that the engine produced.

A pair of Skyraiders (the farther one is visible just below the center of the photo) are conducting a dive-bombing and strafing assault on a Vietcong base adjacent to a canal in the vicinity of Thanh Minh on April 14, 1965. The closer plane has just released what appears to be a napalm bomb from the centerline hard point. *National Museum of the United States Air Force*

A US Air Force Douglas A-1E Skyraider, serial number 52-132421, from the 602nd Fighter Squadron flies over Saigon in 1965. The following year, on July 31, 1966, this plane was serving with the same squadron, renamed the 602nd Air Commando Squadron, when it was shot down by ground forces near Ban Katoi, North Vietnam; the pilot managed to bail out and was rescued by a USAF helicopter crew. *National Museum of the United States Air Force*

To celebrate dropping 6 million pounds of munitions on Communist forces during the first Vietnam War cruise of VA-25, the executive officer of the squadron, Cdr. C. W. "Bill" Stoddard, had a salvaged toilet loaded onto a pylon of his A-1H, "Paper Tiger," side number 572, to release along with the bombs onto Communist forces, on November 4, 1965. According to another Skyraider pilot from VA-25, the toilet-bomb stunt was a sarcastic commentary on the Navy's practice of sending Skyraider crews into harm's way while carrying less than full loads of munitions. Note the VA-25 "Fist of the Fleet" insignia and E-for-efficiency award on the toilet in this prelaunch photo taken on USS *Midway* (CVA-41).

A Republic of Vietnam air force A-1E has just released a general-purpose bomb during an airstrike on Communist forces in a forest in 1965. On the front of the bomb is a fuse extender, designed to detonate the bomb a few feet above the ground. *National Museum of the United States Air Force*

A detachment of US Air Force A-1Es are being serviced at Qui Nhon, Republic of Vietnam, in 1965. Note the very heavy exhaust staining on the side of the closest Skyraider. In the foreground, armorers are preparing bombs; behind them is a flatbed semitrailer loaded with bombs. In the background is a tanker with fuel for the A-1Es. *National Museum of the United States Air Force*

In a photo facing aft from over the windscreen of a USAF Douglas A-1E at Bien Hoa, Republic of Vietnam, in 1965, the pilot is seated in the foreground. Above him, on the center beam of the canopy, is the antenna for the ARN-31 glide-slope and locator receiver, part of the instrument-landing system. The oblong opening in the front of the dorsal fin was the air intake for the environmental-control system for the aft cabin. *National Museum of the United States Air Force*

Douglas A-1J, BuNo 142048, from VA-25, assigned to USS *Midway*, is making a steep bombing run on enemy forces in South Vietnam on November 2, 1965. Eleven just-released Mk. 81 250-pound bombs are visible below the plane.

The Republic of Vietnam air force operated Skyraiders during the Vietnam War, including A-1H, serial number 137607, seen during a mission over the Mekong River delta in May 1966, painted in Southeast Asia (SEA) camouflage of dark green, medium green, and tan, with light gray on the bottom of the aircraft. The national insignia was similar to that of the United States, but with yellow bars with red stripes and edging. The rudder flash was a representation of the Republic of Vietnam flag: yellow with three red horizontal stripes. *National Museum of the United States Air Force*

Douglas A-4 Skyhawks flank the sides of the flight deck of USS *Intrepid* (CVS-11) while Douglas Skyraiders from VA-176 are lined up in the center and rear of the deck during operations at sea on February 18, 1966. Several of the Skyraiders, including the second one and another one on the center of the aft part of the flight deck, have an enormous amount of black exhaust staining on the fuselage.

In the Vietnam War, some of the US Air Force Skyraiders gained immortality as Sandys: armed aircraft that worked closely with USAF search-and-rescue helicopters. During rescue missions, when the helicopters and downed airmen were particularly vulnerable to enemy fire, the Sandys would contend with enemy ground forces, working them over with bombs, rockets, and cannon fire until the helicopters and their crews could extract the downed aircrews. Shown here are two USAF Sandys flying guard over an HH-3C "Jolly Green Giant" on a rescue mission. The nearer Sandy is A-1G, tail number 32619. *National Museum of the United States Air Force*

A USAF A-1E speeds away after dropping a white-phosphorus bomb on Vietcong forces in a mountainous jungle area in 1966. White-phosphorus bombs were used for various purposes, including creating smoke screens and attacking tunnel complexes. Air-to-ground rockets with white-phosphorus payloads also were used in Vietnam. *National Museum of the United States Air Force*

While providing close air support for a rescue mission over North Vietnam in October 1967, a Sandy piloted by Lt. Col. Robert F. Wilke of the 602nd Fighter Squadron (Commando) was hit by enemy fire, tearing up the right flap and part of the wing structure. Wilke was able to fly the Skyraider back to safety, but on January 17, 1968, he was shot down and declared missing in action while attempting another rescue of two downed air crewmen. *National Museum of the United States Air Force*

Posing in front of a US Air Force A-1H, side number 021, at Pleiku Air Base, Republic of Vietnam, on December 18, 1968, are, *left*, Col. George B. Birdsong Jr., commanding officer of the 633rd Special Operations Wing, and Col. Alexander Corey, commander of the 6th Special Operations Squadron. Arrayed in front of the officers and the Skyraider is an ordnance load, including napalm and general-purpose bombs, cluster bombs, rocket pods, and, *in the front*, 20 mm ammunition. *National Museum of the United States Air Force*

Douglas A-1J, BuNo 142046, was transferred to the Republic of Vietnam air force and served successively with the 516th and 520th Squadrons. The aircraft was shot down in combat on June 13, 1968.

A Douglas A-1E, side number 408, is being prepared for takeoff on a mission at Udorn Royal Thai Air Force Base during 1968. Behind the copilot is an ARN-31 antenna. The bombs under the wing are, *left*, an AN/M47A4 100-pound smoke bomb with plasticized white phosphorus (PWP) filling, and an M117 750-pound bomb. *National Museum of the United States Air Force*

Loaded with submunitions dispensers, rocket launchers, Minigun pods, and drop tanks, A-1H, serial number 52-135314, from the 602nd Special Operations Squadron flies a mission in February 1969. On June 18, 1971, this Skyraider was shot down over Ban Na, Plain of Jars, Laos, and the pilot was killed. *National Museum of the United States Air Force*

Aircraft from Carrier Air Wing 1 on the hangar deck of USS *John F. Kennedy* (CVA-67) in 1969 include, *in the foreground*, A-1G (originally AD-5N), BuNo 132575 and side number 751, which is in the process of having its paintwork spot-primed.

Douglas A-1J, BuNo 142064, was one of the Skyraiders turned over to the Republic of Vietnam air force in the 1960s and was photographed at an unidentified airbase in 1969. It is shown in markings for the 516th Fighter Squadron, 41st Tactical Wing, RVNAF.

Painted at an angle on the cowling of an A-1H Skyraider parked in a revetment at Nakhon Phanom Royal Thai Air Base in 1970 is the nickname "Miss Noreen." This plane was assigned to the 22nd Special Operations Squadron "Zorros" and bears the tail code "TS." Faintly visible on the aft fuselage are five tan bands, which identify this as a wing commander's plane. *National Museum of the United States Air Force*

Several Skyraiders, including EA-1F, BuNo 132532, *in the foreground*, are in long-term storage at Davis-Monthan Air Force Base, Arizona, on August 3, 1971. The following year, this EA-1F (originally, AD-5Q) was transported to the National Museum of Naval Aviation, in Pensacola, where it is on static display.

An A-1H Sandy, serial number 52-134609, from the 1st Special Operations Squadron is accompanying a Sikorsky HH-53 Super Jolly Green Giant helicopter from the 40th Aerospace Rescue and Recovery Squadron during a mission in Southeast Asia in October 1972. This plane had the nickname "The Good Buddha" on the side of the cowling. *National Museum of the United States Air Force*

A white Playboy bunny is on a propeller blade of this Skyraider with the "ET" tail code of the 6th Special Operations Squadron, based at Pleiku during the Vietnam War. The plane is loaded with a mix of rocket pods, napalm, and SUU-14A dispensers. *National Museum of the United States Air Force*

Douglas A-1E USAF, serial number 52-132663, served with the 1st Air Commando Squadron, 14th Air Commando Wing. This Skyraider was shot down by antiaircraft fire near Ban Pa Kha, Laos, on October 6, 1967. The pilot was killed in action. *National Museum of the United States Air Force*

A rainbow frames a Douglas A-1E or derivative, side number 445, at an unidentified air base. A number "1" is on the cowling. A mix of bomb types are on the wing pylons. A dark area, likely Engine Gray, is painted on the side of the fuselage to mask exhaust streaks. *National Museum of the United States Air Force*

US Air Force Skyraiders loaded with various types of bombs are lined up at an airfield, date and location unknown. The nearest plane is an A-1G night-attack Skyraider, serial number 52-132548; a red band is painted on the lower part of the main landing-gear door. *National Museum of the United States Air Force*

Although identifying features are sparse in this photo, this Skyraider appears to have been in the service of the Republic of Vietnam. The "VU" tail code is not one used by the US Air Force or Navy. "VU" and the side number "631" appear on the main-gear doors. *National Museum of the United States Air Force*

Two Douglas A-1E Skyraiders are taxiing out of a revetted ramp at a base in Southeast Asia during the Vietnam War while a third Skyraider warms its engine in the left background. Air Force Skyraiders often had the late-type solid-disc wheels as seen on the closest plane, but the early, spoked wheels are on the aircraft to the left. *National Museum of the United States Air Force*

The engine of a USAF A-1E piloted by Maj. Bernard Fisher is starting at Pleiku Air Base, Republic of Vietnam, prior to a mission in 1966. An SUU-11/A Minigun pod is installed on each Mk. 51 pylon. Note the landing light on the left main-gear fairing. Maj. Fisher was awarded the Congressional Medal of Honor for landing in an area overrun by enemy troops to rescue fellow Skyraider pilot D. W. Myers after he was shot down in the A Shau Valley on March 10, 1966. *National Museum of the United States Air Force*

In this close-up of a USAF A-1E, notice the mismatch in the demarcation between the gray and white on the two forward panels of the cowling. The orange pods with fins under the wings appear to have been submunitions or mine dispensers. *National Museum of the United States Air Force*

Ground crewmen with creative drive and time on their hands painted these fanciful schemes on underwing ordnance loaded on Skyraider pylons in Vietnam. Two of the pylons are loaded with clusters of small antipersonnel fragmentation bombs. *National Museum of the United States Air Force*

Douglas EA-1Es (originally, AD-5Ws) are in long-term storage at an unidentified facility. The closer plane, with an "R" on the dorsal fin, appears to have been in the markings of VAW-11, whose tail code was RR. The stripe on the fin also was a VAW-11 marking. *National Museum of the United States Air Force*

A ground crewman assists the pilot in a Skyraider cockpit. On the top of the canopy to the right is an ARN-31 antenna, connected to a receiver for the instrument-landing system, which gave the pilot lateral and glide-slope guidance in making a landing. *National Museum of the United States Air Force*

Only the last three digits, 425, are visible on the tail number of this A-1E with the nickname "Susan 2" on the cowling; this is consistent with USAF serial number 52-132425. The landing light on the left main-gear door suggests this was a USAF plane. *National Museum of the United States Air Force*

Three Skyraiders serving with the Republic of Vietnam air force are flying in formation. The first and second planes are A-1Hs, serial numbers 34498 and 39622. The Republic of Vietnam air force continued to operate Skyraiders up to the time of the Communist takeover of the country in 1975.

An A-1E flies over the Cà Mau Peninsula, at the southernmost tip of the Republic of South Vietnam, in early 1965. From the Korean War to the Vietnam War, the Douglas Skyraider proved to be a tough, durable aircraft in a number of important roles. *National Museum of the United States Air Force*